IN THE GARDEN OF OUR OWN MAKING

IN THE GARDEN OF
OUR OWN MAKING

BARBARA SPERBER

Papier-Mache Press
Watsonville, CA

ISBN: 0-918949-69-6 Softcover

Cover art by Barbara Van Arnam
Cover design by Cynthia Heier
Photo by Steven Sperber

Text from *Verses From 1929 On* by Ogden Nash, copyright ©1936 by Ogden Nash. First appeared in *The New Yorker*. Used by permission of Little, Brown and Company.

Grateful acknowledgment is made to the following publications which first published some of the material in this book:

North Country Anvil, Winter 1981 for "Dream That My Daughter Returns"; *Northern Lit. Quarterly*, Fall 1985 for "My Mother Remembers"; *Hurricane Alice*, vol. 7: 1 and 2, 1990 for "But She Signed the Papers, Didn't She?" (published as "The Birthmother"); *Encodings*, vol. 2, no. 2, 1992 for "Letter from West 112th Street," "Letter from Albert Einstein Hospital in the Bronx," and "Letter from Greenwich Village" (published as "Signing the Papers"); *Pudding Magazine: The International Journal of Applied Poetry*, no. 20, 1993, for "Letter from Brooklyn Heights" (published as "First Love"); and *Poets On:*, vol. 19., no. 2, Summer 1995 for "Songs We Would Rather Know."

Library of Congress Cataloging-in-Publication Data

Sperber, Barbara, 1945–
    In the garden of our own making / Barbara Sperber.
      p. cm.
    ISBN 0-918949-69-6 (softcover : alk. paper)
    1. Mothers and daughters—United States—Poetry. I. Title.
PS3569.P4614I5 1995
811'.54—dc20   95-16436
                                                  CIP

DEDICATION

in memory of my mother

and for Stacey, Jacob, and Rebecca
who have taught me so much

THANKS TO:

Sandra Martz for editorial guidance and her much appreciated interest in my work

Shirley Coe for her availability and steadfast assistance in getting the manuscript into print

a special thanks to Monica Ochtrup for editing this work and for her crucial role in determining its final shape: for finding connections where I thought there were none

my teachers, friends, and family for giving me more than they even know

the members of my writing group, Onion Skins, for helpful criticism and strong support

my husband Steve for making everything possible

CONTENTS

IN THE GARDEN OF OUR OWN MAKING

IN THE GARDEN OF OUR OWN MAKING

INTRODUCTION

On September 10, 1970, I gave birth to a daughter whom I gave up for adoption. Although I actively repressed this momentous event except for an annual letdown on her birthday, the resultant overwhelming emotions tore underneath at my equanimity and stability and surfaced repeatedly in my writing.

Thus began a personal odyssey. During the next fifteen years, I traveled to many places, both geographically and in my mind, carrying my feelings and desires as unpacked baggage. When I delicately opened these bags and contemplated my birth daughter's life, a dam broke within me. I became fascinated with the idea of discovering my daughter's identity and learning what had become of her. Once released from the depths of my repressed psyche, this thought obsessed me, compelling me to search for my daughter. I read Betty Jean Lifton's brilliant, seminal book, *Lost & Found,* which had an overwhelming influence on me and strangely mirrored my own desires and concerns although she was writing about the search for identity from the viewpoint of an adoptee.

I moved frequently during my personal journey, migrating from New York City to Champaign, Illinois, to St. Paul and Princeton, then to Russia, France, and back to St. Paul. One stop on my travels was a small Greenwich Village apartment where the poet Philip Schultz taught a writing class. With a no-nonsense manner, he encouraged me to work from emotion, creating poetry out of the real, burning issues that choreographed my life.

But it wasn't until my husband and two children and I spent six weeks in Moscow (while my husband exchanged ideas with fellow mathematicians) that I was able to write to my birth daughter directly. Feeling safely tucked away in another part of the world— living on the eighth floor of a Stalinist fortresslike dormitory among male graduate students from Cuba, Africa, and Afghanistan (who didn't understand me as I "intoned" down the hall)—I started writing poems directly *to* my daughter, telling her how much I wanted to find her.

When our family returned to the states that September, I repeatedly spent evenings searching birth records at the New York Public Library. Eventually, through a network of birth parents, I discovered my daughter's identity. In December 1987, I drove by her house, and I finally contacted her the following April. A few months later, just as she was turning eighteen, I met my birth daughter as an adult.

Less than a year after I met my daughter face-to-face, my mother learned that she was in the advanced stages of three different kinds of cancer. Two days after my family and I had arrived in Bordeaux on the southwest coast of France, she called from North Carolina to tell me. She encouraged me to stay in Europe, thinking she would surely surmount the disease if she counterpunched hard enough. Since my mother was the gutsiest fighter I knew, I believed she would succeed. After further telephone conversations, I flew from Paris to see her, realizing that she might not hold on. I visited her again four months later, the last time I would be with her.

That final visit with my mother is where this book begins. Sitting with my dying mother in Pinehurst, North Carolina, impelled me to look back at my past and to examine not only the complexity of my relationship with my mother—with all its intense conflict and love—but also the events which caused me to give up my child. (It's intriguing that two of my most intense relationships tested the mother-daughter "synapse.") From there, I was propelled into the future, tracing my search for my daughter, our ensuing reunion, and the integration of this new relationship into my life.

In the Garden of Our Own Making proceeds from loss, moving toward connection. My mother dying and my daughter being born are part of the same life process, and the lost child in each of us emerges at various stages of this process. Integration of loss and desire are the themes of this book, and the shaping of a new kind of love. And while the outward subject matter here is adoption and my dealings with parents and progeny, underneath, the true issue is my own search for identity. This literary undertaking was part of my personal quest to create a new, more entrenched self—the outcome of a difficult journey.

In the Garden of Our Own Making embraces several poetic forms, yet is essentially one continuous narrative progression, telling a story—*like so many other women's stories*—that needs telling. As with a novella, this book should be read, if possible, in one sitting.

Barbara Sperber
April 1995

Vigil: Letter from Pinehurst

PART ONE

i

She wears a cotton nightgown and thin golf sweater,
  but a thick horse blanket

wraps her stick legs propped on the base
  of her green tweed recliner.

Diagonally across from her on the silk brocade sofa,
  I face the floor-to-ceiling windows

that clasp the wall like finite seams, like panels
  stitched to another world.

Outside—the shining lake. Yet I cannot see it, nor she,
  though she stares straight ahead at the dining room mirror.

Usually the mirror reflects the lake in its monster confines,
  giving the illusion in obscene length and breadth

that one's eyes are viewing the water. Today the blinds—
  paper-thin slats especially treated to block out the sun—

demolish the rays as skillfully as steel runners.
  She whispers, "My neighbor owns the company,

installed them himself *at cost.*" (Little did he know
  how kind he was—on this sere, Carolina day,

if air blows in, her cancerous, devoured lungs
   won't exhale or inhale.) Dad putters in to reset

the air-conditioning even lower than I used to beg him
   when years ago, on those deafening days, I'd gasp for breath

(swallowed whole by her chatter). I sit and gaze at her
   and float on the sofa's sheer green-and-pink peacocks.

After drifting away, she opens her eyes, then swims back
   into a short sleep like she's diving into the lake

for quick refreshment (it's the morphine she's taking).

Dad's in his study pushing papers, his pale, high forehead
   bent slightly (the stoic forehead he passed on

to me with grey-green eyes and sun-bleached hair).
   A grandmotherly nurse with a soft southern drawl

and the unlikely name of Christina Craft folds sheets in the kitchen
   and peels potatoes in a chipped, blue bowl with hushed reverence.

I drift toward the kitchen to pour myself tea
   when Christina tells me, "Last night your mother said,

'Please stay over—don't worry, I'll pay you extra,
   and my dear, don't sit in the chair. No, sleep on the sofa

in the living room. It's expensive, but much more comfortable.'
   Can you imagine that?" Christina emphasizes.

"What a generous lady! And in her condition!"
   I can't stop tracking the sun on the lake—

blocked and shunted from me, but solemnly there,
   like an immigrant god about to descend, forcefully,

across the ocean (a mammoth, glacial creature storing fire
   and unexpected violence). I'm waiting for the second

when Dad returns to open the blinds, for a naked view
of the seething sun exploding behind the slats.

I ask Christina, "Do you want tea?"
Her back is turned; I think she's crying.

iii

Taut, wide-eyed, Mother rustles in her chair, then quietly asks me,
  "Any unfinished business?" leaning back in her chair

with the weight of her disease. "No," I say, smiling,
  thinking, *Yes, there will always be unfinished business*

between us—the way there is always silence
  even in the hub of traffic.

The one thing I wanted from her—breathing space—
  she couldn't give, and I wouldn't donate

what she desperately needed—praise, reassurance
  she was doing things right.

But I smile, say, "No," because she's in pain
  and it's hard watching her die—

and because I think I'm the one who's dying.

iv

When I was young and flushed with fever, I remember:
  she sat for hours at the edge of my Ethan Allen bed

and the heart in her tiny sparrow body would beat wildly
  (I realize now) as she waited for me to slough off

my sickness. I could barely feel her fingers on my forehead,
  let alone the planet of her bruised heart.

She cooed, made jokes in her singsong, little girl voice.
  With the most dramatic inflections, she recited Ogden Nash:

"Oh, early every afternoon / I like a temporary swoon.
  I do not overeat at luncheon, / I do not broach the bowl or puncheon;

Yet the hour from two to three / Is always sleepy-time to me."
  She'd give a performance like Sarah Bernhardt

and seem indifferent to my pain and chills. Afterward,
  she'd nervously collapse, want nothing to do with me.

When she'd twitch, shudder, as she passed me in the hall
  (drowned by something she wasn't aware of),

I'd think I was to blame—like a dog who's torn up a carpet,
  but forgets which one, and even the room.

She'd race, as usual, to her lists like a windup toy
    (or a puppet with its heart cut out).

"Should I go bowling? Should I keep my purple dress?
    The salesclerk says I look divine.

And would you massage my back? OOOoooh! How I need it!
    If you do, I'll let you stay up late.

And could you knead my eyebrows? It will help my sinuses."

v

(There are nights I still can't sleep without picturing
   her body—its soft, olive hardness.

These were her breasts: small and firm,
   the skin slightly sallow. At night,

dancing nude in front of the TV when I was trying to watch,
   she paraded them, dripping—crazy from the bath.

When, finally, she jumped into bed, she'd lift her
   sheer, rose nightie midway to her lower back

so her buttocks shone brown in the lamplight.
   Then she begged me to rub—her round face pleading,

her hazel irises burning through my pores. She just
   wanted her back soothed with dips and caresses.

Fingers and nails. Softer—no, harder.
   My practiced hands played her like a keyboard

and the chords strung out into uneven waves,
   blue and melodic, and the bass lines blurred.

This is how, year after year, I helped her
   fall into sleep, coursing past borders

I still can't understand.
  She smacked her lips, she stroked her thigh;

I floated through solids, I sank into air.)

vi

Years later, she said, "Your fevers frightened me.
   I panicked, afraid you wouldn't make it through."

Back then—how could I know? If I tried to speak,
   she ignored me, like a child shut alone in her room,

cut off forever from the country of her feelings.
   "Should we have the Goldmans over?" "Should we play bridge?"

"Should I make paella—or think about it later?"
   "Should I take a nap?" "Do you think I'm tired?"

"Would a drink help me?" *"Do you think I'm tired?"*
   The questions would follow so quickly,

they canceled each other out (nonstop, for days)!
   I'd grow numb. My heart va-voomed. My cheeks would smart

and my chest tighten. I'd float to a brown spot
   on the ceiling—sucked out of time by a giant vacuum.

vii

Now I am the one that anxiously watches over—the mother
    who tends *her* spirit, as she drifts, sideways,

in her dream, and I am the sponge that absorbs *her* pain,
    though I feel a trickle of warmth slip through.

You who bit me with your kisses, squeezed me like soap,
    and stole my air; who drowned me in elephantine desires

to be rubbed and caressed; who could never get enough
    praise and adoration, but gulped it down with martinis

when my fever subsided (an executive privilege
    for the difficult vigil of watching over me);

who pranced up and down, shelving me; who couldn't give me
    honest reassurance that I'd make it through morning,

that I lived in my body: I give it to you now—praise
    and forgiveness for doing things "right,"

the only way you could (and you'll make it through
    to the other side; of that, I've no question).

But know I, too, will brave these hours of watching over you,
    and the fierce ones after you're gone,

though even now—in between snoozes and forays to beyond—
  bursts your usual need to be perfect. In your husky,

low-pitched voice, you ask me—nervous,
  "Darling, will you be all right?

Are you sure?"

PART TWO

i

Soon the sun will set and all this unfinished business
    will slide into darkness, like a canoe slipped quietly

into the lake, but held at bay by a patient hand.
    The living room's contained by its own singularity:

its pure, fractured light stabs the dusk
    and veils our faces in its sharp petals.

We sit across from each other
    like passengers on a night train to Minsk

and sip our tea, Russian style, in tall glasses
    like her father's mother by the River Neman.

The silver coasters glistening beside us,
    we're protected by the rhythm of the wheels,

but weighted down by our separate destinations—
    the bent beams and rails of our past lives.

Can she still hear her mother's voice?
    (And hear her father's fist, see it slam her cheek?)

She's shrunk, reduced to eyes and bone,
    packed to the chin in army green horse blankets.

Her peasant face, no longer round as the moon—
  staccato, demanding—looks elegantly polished,

an Etruscan statue radiating light.
  Her hazel, cavernous eyes are burning through me

in a rain shower of unfinished business.
  "Barbara," she says (fading),

"Please don't be depressed. But if you *can't* help it,
  please save it for *after* I'm gone."

I sip my Red Zinger, suddenly woozy on the sheer sofa
    with its subtle greens and whites and garter belt pinks

tastefully picked by her decorator who loved hues,
    loved *her* even more, more than a son:

he *still* comes to visit. Why am I afraid I'll spill my tea?
    Her equivalent to "peeing on one's dress at a country club luncheon."

(When I'd reminded her of what she'd said, she grew horrified
    that her words had slipped out. Fluting her brows and arching her voice,

like a coy girl caught with her pants down,
    she'd asked me, "Did I *really* say that?")

She drowses again, then opens her eyes, larger
    than I've ever seen them, reminding me of green-brown waves,

the sea in autumn—
    those voids in paintings, impressionist blurs

I almost start to grasp before they sink into earth tones.
    (Yes, she was strangely earthbound.)

iii

When she danced the Charleston, she'd thwack her thigh,
    peering sideways to see if we were watching.

When she didn't crave our faces as mirrors of approval,
    she was shrewd, fiercely practical.

A feisty, loudmouthed fighter. Single-handedly (was I proud!)
    she saved the homes of Blacks in Saddlertown

(hidden in the forest at the end of our street).
    In her ripped yellow T-shirt, she yelled, *"Damn you!"*

to the mayor and school board and used car salesmen
    and neighborhood fanatics; such chutzpah

I could never muster! Yet I remember, year after year
    what she hated and feared the most:

that she'd always be known as "that *poor,*
    dark, little Jewish girl," or was it "that *dark,*

little, poor Jewish girl"? (In her dreams she was surely
    what she needed to be: tall, blond, and *goyishe,*

rich as her college roommate.) Oh how she'd talk,
    reminisce, and juice up the details! My love for rhymes,

sensual language, and gross hyperboles
 could only have come from her (like the moon

must have sprung from the sky).

iv

Now life takes on the shades of the living room.
The fading sun I still can't see.

The reflected light's bounced painfully back,
as on the walls of Plato's cave—

puppet shadows, shadows of shadows.
Yet somehow I feel the sun which creeps at last

through the slats of the blinds. The gargantuan mirror
punctiliously tacked on the dining room wall behind my back

will soon blaze intensely, like Monet's paintings of the ocean
at Argenteuil, where light burns through the sea

and life through the moment (as if finally lifted out of itself,
raised from the dark by the blade

of its pure transparency—*a god's wing on fire*).

V

Is *this* the final moment—when Dad putters in
　　to open the blinds? Swish! I can almost hear it.

The sharpened light spilling through the glass
　　like love itself (her eyes buried beneath her almond-shaped lids).

My thirst for her to tell me that she loves me
　　is also buried.

My inner life, hidden from her, and all those silent countries—
　　Mississippi in the '60s, and Russia, too, where I longed

to escape; and further back in time—that other recessed state,
　　where I cry,

"Don't leave me. Don't leave me." (What I fear
　　and crave the most). I didn't choose this frame

of her going—the almost-slain sun striping the room
　　like a transparent bandage.

vi

Back from his study, Dad walks in, settled in his pain
    like a rower in his makeshift boat,

not allowing himself to show it—smiling, chatting,
    though he's usually quiet (which makes him seem devout).

I can see now the shimmering longleaf pines shaking briskly
    in the hot wind, so white they seem frozen

(swaying icicles on Christmas morning). Christina comes
    to hand Mother pills. Mother strains forward

to check her *own* tally, neatly marked in clear red ink
    in rows of five (even spaces between them).

"Christina! You've forgotten the tamoxifen!
    It must also be given at seven. The doctor left

special instructions; don't you remember?"
    Christina motions me into the bedroom. "My dear," she says,

blue eyes squinched, "She told me how much you love words—
    you should write a poem. Now any other woman

would snore six feet under, but *she* keeps going."

vii

The doorbell. Another of her newfound Christian friends
   (miles from Flatbush) breaking the silence

that rips through the drifts in the lake and my own
   plunging thoughts. It slices her immersion in sleep;

her lids flutter. Then her green-gold eyes illuminate
   her sunken cheeks... she is almost gone

(her suffering, too, about to end).
   Another phone call. I run to answer.

The portable phone next to her chair, somehow,
   is mysteriously missing. So I race to the kitchen phone,

wondering, *Does she want to talk?* (She still gets upset
   if I don't check). But there's no difference now

between waking and sleeping. We both feel it.
   We both know it. It's how she used to say,

when she tried to pound sense into me,
   "That's just how life is, you'd better get used to it."

viii

This final curve between waking and sleeping reminds me
    of my firstborn daughter—when we slept together

on her first day in the world—before I gave her up
    for adoption. When I lay propped on pillows in my bed

overlooking the Bronx River Parkway. When they placed her
    in the nook of my elbow, and we rested, oh, so peacefully—

rocked in our boat, back and forth, she and me
    (between then and now). With her wide, sweet mouth

she sucked her bottle, and I stroked the down on her scalp,
    and the world was our cradle—the two of us

drifting in and out of sleep—sinfully, cosmically
    happy. Now Mother, too, drifts, but pulled by morphine

and cradled by a different knowledge (and shoots and streaks
    of snaking pain, as she tosses on an infinite ocean).

Yes, she's leaving for good, but not in the way
    I'd imagined. As I say good-bye, a part of me

is also leaving.

ix

I reach for her hand to kiss her fingers,
    but she motions me away (afraid of showing too much,

floods of feeling she can't control). Yet I understand,
    in her worried way: as usual,

she thinks she's protecting me from pain—that last church,
    the final fortress that I need protection from.

There are no more flickering shadows or giant feathers
    of light encasing colonial vases and bookshelves

like gossamer wings. Only the arc of the lamps,
    glittering circles in their subdued planets.

Only this monochrome brightness (light kills dark
    and dark kills light in a room without any shadings).

Dad slides open the windows. I rise to pour more tea.
    In the mirror, I can see a party boat

skimming the lake in the near distance. I can hear
    fistfuls of laughter: a woman in the boat

is rocking, singing, singing for us all
in her pure, husky way. Her voice

reaches me in waves—from her separate space
to my separate spaces.

WE ENTER THE WORLD

LETTER FROM BROOKLYN HEIGHTS

1.

In my daffodil dress I shield you from the gaze of strangers. Its
V neck is narrower than V's I'm used to, but it swims much deeper,
heightening the sheen in my skin. It's winter. He drinks with sailors
outside Montero's, and when light returns through the bars on our
windows, he swerves home in elephant rage and stomps the floor-
boards—threatens to kill me if I speak, or breathe. But this morning,
it shot right through me, like a girded prong in my upper chest. This
red, crushing nausea! No matter that it made me heave, I felt your
power as if you had embraced me. I straddled down Montague to
the Promenade and viewed the outlines of lower Manhattan—win-
dows that pave the soot of the sky—and welcomed you, child, as *a
separate being*.

LETTER FROM BROOKLYN HEIGHTS

2.

Even on the north side of Hicks Street, it starts to warm. A junkie
hauls his take down the next-door fire escape. Hookers solicit
more rashly than common. Though the rivers on the streets are no
longer slippery, neither he nor I can walk on our own—he needs
drink, I succor.

   In the mornings on the way to the bodega, I sway downstairs
and my heart va-vooms. Then my knees lock, and the sky tilts and
the brownstones blur. The muscles tighten in my legs (like screws
on the ships across from Montero's preparing to leave). He downs
eggs in a dingy cabin with some zonked seaman. Floating or try-
ing to "talk in tongues" or quoting Hegel, he quietly passes out.

LETTER FROM BROOKLYN HEIGHTS

3.

Today when he lost his job for bourbon on his breath, he drove fear
into my palpitating body—hating me, but himself more—as if diving
into waters with sharks and piranhas. Then he shoved me out the car
(though I'm five months pregnant). Later in the evening, bending
low to the broiler, I turned the pork chops. My pilot flame blew—a
light flashed on! I decided to leave for good. Not caring for my life, I
hoarded yours, afraid of what he'd do five years later.

LETTER FROM BROOKLYN HEIGHTS

4.

When he yells or when I walk on the sidewalk, my knees jam. I grow
hot, dizzy, certain I'll faint, that the streets will swallow me whole.
Petrified of my own heartbeat, I don't exist or live in my body.

I want to keep you, hold you forever. Can't earn a living. Can't
breathe the air. Can't pass an hour or go to buy groceries without
panicking that I'll die. That the city, too, will disappear.

Can't love myself enough to unclench my fists or trudge out the
door for good. But go to the doctor who hands me pills.

When he tells me he won't help me—unless I give you up—I cry,
No. Never. Never. Never. Never. Claw and roar. Weep and bleed.

LETTER SPEEDING UP THE WEST SIDE HIGHWAY

The sun arrives like an icon. The alarm clock explodes. I collect
clothes and a Japanese diary with white chrysanthemums streaking
the cover. While he snores, I sneak from the apartment like an angel,
or prisoner. Then I hail a cab and whisk myself in, bloated as a por-
poise. Yet grief is kind—the marrow of my love. I'm pulled by your
deepening rhythms, cradled by the length of your pearly limbs,
already so close, becoming human.

Soon I stretch a mattress on the slippery rug of a one-time
friend's room, and trace you with the pads of my fingers—familiar
but foreign in the shaded light.

LETTER FROM WEST 112TH STREET

1.

At night, ten flights high, my chin on the window ledge, I rock you before you are born. I can't picture you, only what I'd do with you: On the playground I brush off your trousers and soothe your knees in the caves of my hands. Leaving your father was easier than dreaming (scooting out the door, suitcase in tow).

LETTER FROM WEST 112TH STREET

2.

The West Side swells in June by Riverside Drive. A tan businessman
dallies in flowers. The bag lady, who used to hug me, drinks in the
sun by the foot of a statue. My yellow dress fills out more than ever,
polishing my skin, sheer as diamonds. I shift from raw, breaking love
to full, unbending despair and watch you paddle in my depths—
feeling rudely sexual, like the pelicans I saw mating at the zoo.

LETTER FROM WEST 112TH STREET

3.

Alone these last, squat months, I ride the bus down Amsterdam Avenue from 110th Street, and watch the street kids spin on the hydrants—in July, the only source of water to cool their spirits or baptize their longing. Then I ring the bell of the agency—a married, divorcing woman, no teenage pariah behind closed doors of some obscene religious mansion where nuns stream the halls, grinning with puffed-out cheeks.

These hours you float in my body, I question your fate, the way the earth must question the sky, alone at night, when spaces grow immense. In dreams I sign the papers, rip them, and sign them again, and trembling, leave the room. *Give up* is a strange phrase— exotic for a mother.

LETTER FROM MOOSE LAKE

August, a month before your birth. Garbage collectors circle, on strike. Armies of maggots topple the cat's dish. The elevator's broken—and the phone. For three days the mercury strikes one hundred.

To escape the dog shit, exhaustion, I ride to a lake north of the city, then push myself out to the middle of the water. Stroking and sinking, I try again (conjuring your cheek, smooth as a willow). I curse the sea, try to anchor. I call your name—Ebba, from a German novel, serene lady-in-waiting to the princess at court. My child, love is not sufficient. I can barely tread water.

Here, in the tracks of the current—invisible layers beneath the surface—I give you to the unknowing air. I relinquish your name.

I'll sign the goddamn papers. Then I swim back to shore.

LETTER FROM GREENWICH VILLAGE

My fingers bloom swollen. I couldn't wear a wedding ring even if I wanted to. I swoon up the stairs of my sixth-floor walk-up, bleary from the day. Suddenly I notice bright, white spots circling the room like planets out of whack. Now the white lights are splashing, bumping into each other like seals in a circus. I don't hold your body. I don't own the world—only white on white, my thin life blinking.

MY MOTHER REMEMBERS

Later, when we could afford a child,
the boiler burst.
In the kitchen it reached forty-two
only when we were lucky.
Three months pregnant, I biked to court,
trying to shame the landlord into burning the oil,
but the judge was a friend of the landlord's
and used the war to cut expenses,
said, "Lady, go home and have your baby."

I pedaled to our fifth-floor walk-up,
then, running up the stairs,
I heard, suddenly, the screech of a faucet.
I screamed: I was the faucet.
If I moved, you would slip out.

Through summer, Dad emptied bedpans.
My hair grew long as Rapunzel's.
I stayed in bed, stirring casserole surprise,
reading Tolstoy in my slip
to the ancient noise of Flatbush.

It was difficult.
I lay waiting for six prone months.
The braids toppled from my head
like layers of the earth.
I was sore, open.
I feared you'd come too quickly
or you wouldn't come out at all
as a shape I would call human.

But when you came,
the opening stretched further
than I would have believed possible.

Such a small space
shifting into valleys and rivers,
then zip, the rip was so quick
when you flew into this world.
I called, "Nurse, help me.
I'm doing a bowel movement."
Then, in the 1940s,
we didn't know what to expect,
how to "go with the pain" like an airplane ride
or a midnight swim under the water,
how to stop only to catch our breath
as we tore apart from shoulder to shoulder.

We couldn't take our husbands
into the room with us.
You swam, bloody in me,
for six bold months,
so that finally, when you split
from my body
through the skin and gristle,
through the bowel and vagina,
it felt like the Allies
sweeping over Europe.

Once outside, you wailed,
malnourished.

I had prayed that the heaviness
would leave me.
And the war had just ended.
But in those days, I cried out in sleep
in the twilight doze that the doctors induced
for three purple nights,
to awake, finally, to the Cold War
and the scent of your frail, cool body.
Your buttocks caved in instead of out.
Your legs bent like chicken wings.

LETTER FROM ALBERT EINSTEIN HOSPITAL IN THE BRONX

1.

No one comes to stay with me in labor. No one explains anything. Wheeled to emergency, I still see white. I hear a voice: "Blood pressure, 200." At two A.M., when my waters break, a blond night nurse (a courier of God) asks me gently, "Do you know what's happening?" I don't—through the ponds of medication—but feel her fingers lift me from below. Framed by gas, I push toward your coming. You are pulled through, but I can't see you.

Later, I shine in fever. I think the bed has flown to Fairbanks. My legs dance "Begin the Beguine" through blue layers of snow. The floorboards whisper I'll never make it.

LETTER FROM ALBERT EINSTEIN HOSPITAL IN THE BRONX

2.

The day nurse whispers, "She has the smoothest features of any new-born in the nursery." You're fat, calm, voluptueuse, as Baudelaire imagined rich, foreign countries—lands not just for the spirit, but the flesh of this world, which stays behind to grieve in daylight when the loved one leaves.

At feeding times you dawdle in the nursery. Svelte, rouged nurses tickle you awake; I can no longer feed you. *The pleasure is too intense.*

I leave the hospital, belly bloated, kidneys like pigs' ears, and check myself in at a stone hotel off East Eleventh Street—the wind of your sucking long since gone, drowning the rain at Washington Square.

LETTER FROM GREENWICH VILLAGE

At night, I feel the waves lapping beneath the birth exhilaration.
They bundle in. They clamor out. Sinking, yet high on this life—
one could say on your "prenatal" spirit, your delicate chutzpah to
survive the city and miraculously blossom—I shift westward
slowly down Eighth Street, noticing families dallying in rain, and
wait to sign the papers, the hem of my daffodil dress swirling
gently. *We enter the world.*

The Road Stretches Out

SOLOMON'S MOTHERS

"The women we have worked with have struggled to understand the intense bond they feel for a child whom they know only as a memory or fantasy."

Millen, Leverett, and Samuel Roll, "Solomon's Mothers: A Special Case of Pathological Bereavement." *American Journal of Orthopsychiatry*, vol. 55, no. 3, July 1985: 411–418.

BUT SHE SIGNED THE PAPERS, DIDN'T SHE?

Every two months she keeps on
having this dream: she smarts
with thirst and excitement
just as if her milk were
letting down. She feels
the rivers in her ducts deep
inside her chest
and aches in the caverns
of her glands to the
boundaries of her skin
and can smell the bluish milk
rippling, tingling,
pumping wildly, but it won't
let down. It stops, just
hangs there, blocked at the
border, pressed against her
flesh, and her breasts swell,
molten, on fire. Her
soul constricts tighter,
smaller—yet she feels
the milk oozing toward the
surface, skimming over tissue,
begging to be free. She can
taste the milk, there's no
other way to say it; in the
morning light, she tastes the milk.

"THEN WHY DID YOU GIVE HER UP
IN THE FIRST PLACE?"

You buy yourself gladiolus
today to celebrate—
from the St. Paul farmer's market,
two dollars a bunch.

They shoot straight up,
all the bright colors.
The stems, bolder
than penises, thrust
nakedly into space

(and lettuce fresh
from the earth
and very yellow wax beans).

Then you walk down Grand
as far as you can go

and remember the Bronx...

standing at the semiprivate window,
looking over the Expressway
and finding the trees
then noticing the river, as you held her

in your arms, in your
peach nightgown, wearing
no black eyeliner...

and remember the world,
so so sad,
but the two of you
somehow complete;

you could say, *sinfully*
happy—

separate, together.

DREAM THAT MY DAUGHTER RETURNS

My daughter comes back to me.
She is ten, though I think
she is five. Her face dark,
though I know she is fair.
A young girl takes care of her,
brings her to school.

I'm only allowed to watch.

I plot to take possession
as if she were a stopwatch
inadvertently left in a pawnshop.
She leans over my shoulder and reminds me
that no one is perfect.

Maybe Grandfather will help win her back.
He is senile, but he used to be a lawyer.
She pries open a nut,
as serious as a squirrel.
The leaves are turning on the vines
that overhang the fences.

EACH LIKE ME,
EACH DIFFERENT

I read their stories.
Each is like me,
each different.
Rich and poor girls,
nice, "squeaky clean
girls," and the girls
"you'd always known
would get into trouble"—
the silent constituency
I never dreamed of

to which I belonged.
An invisible league
of women,
no member learning
the others existed.
But each with the same
salt loads twisting
down her cheek
in hidden rivers.

Each with the same
face, viewed only
in a cloaked mirror.

Each with the face-
within-the-face
twined in worry
for the lost child.

HOW IT'S DONE

You call your college roommate in New York, who
phones the man she used to date, who
helps people search, whose own birth father,
a deceased lawyer, forty years before
doctored his records—so no one could
find him, nor he them. Now he helps
hundreds over the country match up
with their lost mate. He calls her back
and gives her a number. She calls you
from work. You call a woman who
gives you a name, who gives you
another, who gives you another...
who offers to find your daughter,
no questions answered, who knows
someone who works somewhere with
access to records (who can look up
her file): a person whom you'll
never see, never hear from,
who offers to find her for a fee,
who can save your last stab at paradise.

UPON LEARNING HER NAME

At the end of December,
I pick up the phone.

It's like finding out
I've never been born,

that the grey
in my left eye is really

brown, that God
truly loves me—

either all
or none of the above.

WHILE DRIVING WEST

whereupon
while driving back to St. Paul,
we are rerouted due
to construction
and *accidentally*
pass through the main street
of the small town in Pennsylvania
where she lives
and I see
her house—
white and green,
situated on a beautiful
lake
with the sun sinking slowly
behind it,
and I realize suddenly
that she *has*
a mother.

TUCKED BETWEEN
THE JUNK MAIL AND BILLS

I find a letter
postmarked New Jersey.

"...I always thought
if I came upon

your picture,
if I saw your face—

I'd feel unearthly,
but I don't—

I just
feel happy."

A MAN AND HIS WIFE

(the week before I meet her)
for Suzanne and Steven

I can't sleep nights and picture
her parents curled
inside their sheets like geese

    at the water's edge. They slide
    downstream on their double
    mattress, as *she* floats, singly,

away. Her fingers press
against the curve of his spine.
His shoulder braces. Her knee's

    pulled high. Her thin, white cheek
    fans his elbow. His right lid
    blinks at five in the morning.

In the haze, his jaw is clenched,
but her mouth stays slightly
open. Does she see something pass—

    a leaf? a stem? a face in the water?
    They need *her* to want them;
    want *her* to need them. I love them

for that. The current's pulling,
gathering steam. I dream
that *she* turns, swims slowly back.

FLIGHT

"The scariest day of my life,"
I tell her—the blond
with the French chignon
who presses into my elbow
(she's sipping vodka, skimming
Town and Country).

"Really?" she says with a slight
Norwegian accent as she flips
the pages.

    "But the most exciting!"

I try to explain, but omit
how I lost her when I couldn't
walk on my own without spinning
or jamming at the knees—
and no husband to measure my
flight or steady my elbow.

I keep in the pain
and dizziness of search;
how I sped out the letter
at my mother's house
in the southern dawn
when the golfers snored
and the grits weren't boiling yet.

Suddenly I spot one jagged
tear slide from her sapphire eye.

Soon, it mysteriously disappears.
Her right eyebrow stretches
even higher.

"I'll be thinking of you both
at five o'clock exactly.
Yes, I wish you good luck,
the two of you."

She turns to read, drinking
in the pages like she sees
an object of inner recognition,
then slips from my life
like a rowboat down a fjord.

COMING DOWN FROM THE CLOUDS

1.

Zonked from not sleeping
(two days awake
and four flights later),

I'm bringing her back.
We're up in the air.
I'm gazing at magenta clouds,

shiny, dense as a newborn's
cheek. I say, "But they're so
beautiful!" thinking *she*

and I and he could have been
so beautiful! I'm watching
her calm smile, her inscrutable

dazed eyes. Light pierces
our grey metallic trays.
I ask, "Do ya want gum?"

This simple question seems
like a privilege not granted me
on earth. "Sure," she answers,

tired of blushing.
I ask myself, in the last
seven minutes, have I stopped

repeating that I've always
loved her? That a day
hasn't passed when I haven't

thought of her?
I sip my tea.
She chews in silent wonder.

Light strikes the tips
of our knees and the borders
of our fingers. *I swear we're dying.*

COMING DOWN FROM THE CLOUDS

2.

We roam the downtown streets,
circling the blocks like horses

in a ring. Round and round
we go in love, but I can't find

the number three bus I've hailed
time and time before. I say,

"Fuck. Shit. Goddamn,"
peering sideways to see if she

can take it. Suddenly I can't
stop cursing, can't stop tides

stored from years of circling
without direction.

"I don't give a fuck
if we ever make it home."

She laughs her mysterious laugh.
Then we spot the Burger King—

now a useless constellation
though it frames the bus stop.

Shooting past it toward the
Landmark Cafe, I nudge her

to enter. We order, settle in,
poke at our eggs like children,

latching on to each other's voices
as if our lives depended on it.

She tells her tales and I, mine:
the pitch and yaw that lay buried

for years. The words scatter,
spread gently around us

like wildflowers
on the hard, smudged floor.

THIS TIME

As the "natural"
mother,
I read
I could be jailed
for this:

in Roman times
they could
prick
out my tongue
for trying
to find her
or speak to her
or touch

as I touch
her now,
fold my skin
around hers,
framing
her shoulder
in the crevices
of my hand,

my side up
against her,
our waists
brushing.

For our time
together,
there are no
precedents.

HIGH ON GRAND AVENUE

Shy as each other, her father,
or mine, we walk, find nothing
to say. Clouds melt like butter,
the sun slides down. Look!
The buses ride faster. My heart
zooms harder as we cross St. Albans,
and sky darkens quicker through lace
in the windows, and legs of the antique
marble dressers glisten like snake eyes.

There is something about soaring,
in love, like dropping into a steep,
gritty pit, with no rope to lean on
or shimmy up at uneven intervals,
but liking the dark, its sleek
petaled shelter—looking up at the world
from deep down below, and also on top,
on the aging sidewalk—we glide,
together, again.

DRIVING ST. PAUL

I love the way light
cages everything we see.
How softly it offers its arms
to the trees as we zip
in my grey Toyota!

> *This morning, steps*
> *look like steps. Sky*
> *tastes like sky. This bagel*
> *breathes like a bagel.*
> *The road stretches out*
> *like the moment of birth.*

When love coiled underground,
this street ran topsy-
turvy. Elm roots stretched,
then disappeared, higher
than the cloying leaves.

Cats backtracked
in full range of squirrels,
couldn't grasp snow;
their claws wouldn't cling.

> *But today along Lexington,*
> *porches rise, boundless.*
> *A lawn swing sways like*
> *a lawn swing. A tabby*
> *squats slowly to the earth.*

I shift gears.
She runs
to click pictures,
blinding dormers
along Summit Avenue.

Nothing compares to this light
trapped forever
in the present tense.

AFTER HER VISIT

Life returns. The sprinkler
on the maple, the flushed kid
at the park, dank cement
by Breugger's Bagel Bakery.
Retractable sky too taut
to turn blue.

The bitchy neighbor. Her
mauve, soaked roses. The wauling
of her cat *not* screwing
more piercing than a thousand
cats in heat.

The empty mailbox with no
repeat-letter inside from her.
No scrawl, no lousy penmanship
just like mine on ripped
notebook paper, saying again:

"I always thought if I
came upon your picture,
if I saw your face—
I'd feel unearthly,
but I don't—
I just feel happy."

As if once weren't enough
and faith insufficient.
As if I could lose her again
and she'd need to bless me
over and over.

No, the clouds aren't *really*
suicidal or the trees
tense, deciduous.
Hell, I have my own life too,
and she, hers;
that's starkly apparent.

THIS OR THAT

You ask yourself if *this* or *that*
is helpful, like Contac for a cold
or a new mix of plaster for the pipe
curling in the basement.

Does she find your love soothing
like a photo in just the right album,
mounted in the perfect place;
or is it pleasant gibberish

like the cardinal's chatter in the
backwoods of childhood where she
roamed for days—scratching out
leaves, sticks, and bottle caps

to mount her fortress and map
her existence? Is love practical?
Can it salve wounds, open up
pain—the edges of shyness,

the sweet song of sex? And can it
make her happy, like a choir of light
spreading in leaves—springing
out of nowhere, like an honest poem?

DOING IT RIGHT

Suddenly, for no reason,
sipping coffee, munching a bagel,
I hear the pitch of her voice
the day she left to fly home
to New Jersey. "Barbara,"
she said in her factual
tone with its clear crescendo,
"Barbara, I think you did it
right—I mean finding me
and writing when I turned eighteen.
You know, it was perfect
timing, though you said your
friends advised you different—
said wait until I'm twenty,
and first, you have to write
my parents. But me, well
personally, I think you did it
right—if you want my opinion."

AT COMO LAKE

(The Coldest Day)

No letters, phone calls, address
from her. Light, coiled inside snow,
smatters into fierce jewels.
Windows repeat the stars
at the borders of my trousers.

Day's already dim, sun blinding,
low in the sky; she should see me
circling the water. A wee bit stark,
a wee bit crazy (a smidgen
zealous like our poet Bly),

I'm wondering how light refracts
through windows of her city.
I'm hoping it caresses her cheek
and wraps her bones like a winter
towel when she smarts, exposed

to family and friends. Do their tongues
still cluck when she walks
with her boyfriend? Do their doors
slam tight? Does his black skin
light her sky with beams of wisdom?

Is she learning to save the light?
Is light different than before I met her?
Here in St. Paul, it's pewter
dark. I track her voice
but can't make out the words.

MINNEHAHA PARKWAY IN OCTOBER

The leaves, redder this year,
hang on the trees like curling rice paper.

This year, there are more of them—
more clotting veins and broken capillaries

like an old woman's skin
ripped into a million pieces

or a stained bodice from a youthful party.

This year, there are more crushed angels
crumbling in air, littering the ground.

I can hardly stand it.
The leaves are burning through me.

STEPPING OUT

Daughter—

I received your photo,
the salmon jersey
bunched loosely
on your shoulders,
the white stretch jeans
branching softly
at your hips.
I picture you
burning into womanhood,
eyes level, straight
ahead, but lined
in moist excitement,
the old life swirling
around you like leaves
to be swept away.
Wearing flat heels,
you balance perfectly
and tread lightly
like you know where you're going.

In the Garden of Our Own Making

LETTERS FROM BORDEAUX

1. 34 Rue du Haillan

Hungry for her
I wake
forgetting I've found her.

I want my daughter back,

as close as the air I breathe
as the chee's of the birds
before I hear them

as the workman's drill
through my closed shutter—
his soft, Algerian face
miles from Sétif
as he excavates stones
piled by my door.

Now I'm awake,
I remind myself gently,
jerking on my shorts.

I lurch down Marc Nouaux
toward President Wilson Boulevard
and enter the *tabac*
with three francs for coffee.

I perch and scrawl a mouth,
dizzy for knowledge—
who she's seeing,
what colors she wears.

It's spring in Bordeaux,
birds napping
in their womb of twigs,
air dense and tropical,
the croissant crisp,
espresso cheap.

LETTERS FROM BORDEAUX

2. Where It Counts

But I can't forget his smile—
the young Algerian.
When I asked him yesterday
as I locked my door,
"Are you French?"
he shook his head, sardonic,
though usually he's shy.

"Not here," he said in perfect
French, pressing his
forefinger along the skin
between his wrist and elbow.
"Not here, where it counts."

Spinning from the heat,
I retrace my steps
and offer him a beer—
his black eyes bulbs
of light, his eyebrows
thick as his mother's hair.

Leaning on his shovel,
he thanks me
as the cloudburst breaks.

Suddenly I realize *she's*
always with me, even on this
gutted street in France—
as his country
is always with him;
he wears its pain
and owns his beauty.

LETTERS FROM BORDEAUX

3. The Art of Women Walking

Their eyes, subtly lined,
are moist and glazed
as if they're gazing
into rivers
of their own making.

A taut southern light
frames their faces.
They stare straight ahead
down clean stone streets,
catch buses, do shopping,
their bodies silent
in lace-patterned stockings.

Yet inside, the lining
of their cheeks must sting
from some dazed afternoon
when a lover left them,
or their mother wheezed,
dying, and they bent
to kiss her,
a licorice odor
lingering on their lips.

They walk with
no apparent mystery,
but their passion leaks
softly from within
and dizzies the pavement.

I trail behind them
like a spy,
gleaning the remnants
of their buried lives,
and remember when I found her
as I walked Manhattan,
my face, too, a mask—

how I stepped on the cracks
of the sidewalk,
something as children
we were told not to do,

how I cried in the silence
when I learned her name
though the crowds flew by
on their stylish wings.

LETTERS FROM BORDEAUX

4. The End of the Search

Tonight there's a thin slice of light
over the Dordogne. We drive on the high,

winding path, thinner than a gargoyle's
waist. This spinning makes me dizzy,

cuts through my spleen. Circling
and circling, we spot, finally, the main road

and more incredible, the mirage—the fantastic castle
looming over the cliff.

Then, warm and sinewy and silver,
a jutting angel spreads her wings,

setting us free, real as she or I,
as the day that I found her

cities away over endless fields,
the syllables of her name

rising from my throat
like the moon over Périgord.

LETTERS FROM BORDEAUX

5. My Neighbor, Marie-Antoinette

Her fingers pressed together tight
like the blade of a guillotine,
she spliced the air, pretending
to slice off her head
as if in the past she *had*
been a queen (her white, sparkling
hair cropped short and close).
That was the day I met her.

This morning she knocks and asks,
"Have you seen my cat, Minou?
Perhaps she's hiding in your basement?"

For two months, hour after hour,
I've heard her voice slice
through my garden—a birdlike hoot
like that desperate dove
tracking its mate in the Roman ruins,
a flitter of wing on a crumbling wall.

"Minn-oo-ooo! Minn-oo-ooo!"

I'm in my nightgown,
draped in sleep,
longing for *her* eyes.

"Minou! Minou is back!
Elle a prise au piège un amour."

I can't make out the words
except for one, *sexe*.
Her French is different
than any I've heard,
rumbling off her old,
cracking lips
in canons of consonants.

Marie's black eyes,
oh, how they shine—
like mine, I'm sure,
that day I found *her*—
swimming with flames
that spore and seed
in the twilight.

For all she has in the world
is Minou, who hides
each day, teases,
then returns (tawny fur ball
glistening through trees),
leaping over bushes
to a new life
in her overrun garden—
and then into mine.

She can't find love
until she finds Minou.

LETTERS FROM BORDEAUX

6. In My Garden

So this is paradise *inverted:*
needing to find her over and over,
when I don't know where she is.

I slump on this grey stone bench,
examine anemones and a wild rose
skeining into layers of tangled,

curling moss—like love twined
in its labyrinth of cloud-
doused days. My god, there are

times when I crave only what
I *think* I need: her presence,
like a boat that longs for waves,

gentle rocking, the tilt of the mast.
Other moments my love's pinned down,
anchored by thick, strong ropes

like beautiful, white snakes,
perhaps someday to set sail,
but not before *she calls.*

But my finest hours I hoard
my love for my daughter
whenever she needs it,

the way the ocean
stockpiles foam.
Thirty miles away,

the sea at Arcachon
extends toward light
and glints and hues,

becoming what it
needs to be,
gathering in soil,

for earth's its home
and stars and space
and *even silence.*

LETTERS FROM BORDEAUX

7. Just As It Is

    Leaning out
over my garden, I notice the wisteria stretching   .

    toward my roof.
A turtle named Balthazar camps in the mud,

    swoons, lazily, in the weeds.
Close by, the park's crammed with sliding voices.

    Battery-fed cars zoom
around a track. Children press and steer, their eyes

    on fire, melting
into dark rivers . . . . the sun dips down

    to the fringes of my shutters.
I can almost kiss the sky, and my cobblestone street bends

    toward the nape of the city—
four plazas where vendors roam, creeping out from their

    musky rooms, to unfurl, like flags
onto the streets.

    Dazed, excited
(scared), from moment to moment not knowing

    what will happen,
I breathe the world just as it is:

    this pink, jeweled music—here
and gone.

NEWS FROM AMERICA

for my mother

I raise my glass of St. Emilion
in sun-blanched valleys,
on sand dunes and sunken beaches,

at the edges of cafés
in southwest France
on split, worn streets

piled high with stones
until my craving merges
with the sun, and I sip the rays

from the shifting horizon.
Wanting to drown,
I toast to life

as I once stretched out my arms
to you,
who are now leaving,

and remember how you bent down
to lift me, your cool breath
spearing my cheek

when I still believed
that your hands flew for me—
warm, brown birds, like human songs.

SONGS WE WOULD RATHER KNOW

(Bures-sur-Yvette)

The dog shifts, breathes in slightly,
grey beard bobbing,
guarding the entrance
of Le Sports Café as if his life
depended on it. At the bar
les hommes shake hands, lost
in reflections of breasts and thighs
until he moans, again and again—
half-howl, half-mass for the dead.
The bar springs to life,
dives into action. Laugh lines rise
like mountains in the mist. The men
walk softly to him, soothe his scalp
in their callused hands. Oh, to be a dog:
wanting, with unmasked eyes
instead of sitting, sipping coffee,
and dreaming of the dying!
To inhabit his hot, tan body—
strands of hair straggling
down my cheek. To breathe in
the cigarettes and river of leaves
wafting in from the trees by the church
across the square—those fractured realms
of God and religion;
to yowl and squall,
yes, to draw such love!

IN THE GARDEN OF OUR OWN MAKING

(Pinehurst, North Carolina)

I visit one bright day in June.
I've flown in from Paris.
She greets me at the door,
pretends she's not dying. I see
her shadow. She's smaller. Her chest
heaves, but her ribs are still hidden.

It's splendid through her floor-
length window. Pines look down on her
like a good father from another
life. The lake's aglimmer with green
stripes and hundreds of fishes.
Gold bands thicken the dark waters.

By the side of the house a turtle
banks in prime glazed mud, like a
model in children's clay. She falls
in her chair. It's near
twilight. Outside, the deck is cool
but inside, she's burning.
The lake's aflicker.

Party boats skim in the distance.
Now, in death, we are finally
together. She holds my hand,
her little girl face cupped
by a beam of sun. We are almost
in the garden of our own making,
hearing humming noises, songs
of affection like circling birds.

ABOUT THE AUTHOR

Barbara Sperber holds an M.A. in English and creative writing from the University of Minnesota and an M.A. in early childhood education from the University of Illinois. She has taught writing at the University of Minnesota, Somerville Community College in Somerset, New Jersey, and the College of Associated Arts in St. Paul. She has also worked as a nursery school teacher, a parent educator, and a social worker.

Ms. Sperber has been awarded an Academy of American Poets Prize from the University of Minnesota and an Emily M. Hills Prize for Poetry from Case-Western Reserve University. She also won honorable mention in 1993 for the Helen Wade Roberts Award from the Academic and Arts Press and first prize in the 1995 American Association of University Women's Poetry Contest, sponsored by the St. Paul Chapter. She has published widely in literary journals and small press magazines throughout the country, including *Milkweed Chronicle, Poets On:, Another Chicago Magazine, Encodings, Great River Review, Pudding Magazine: The International Journal of Applied Poetry, Sing Heavenly Muse, Hurricane Alice,* and *The Lake Street Review.* She is a member of the Associate Writing Programs, the Poetry Society of America, and the Academy of American Poets.

Ms. Sperber is currently working on a new collection of poems and a book of short stories. She lives in St. Paul, Minnesota, with her husband, Steven, a mathematician, and her children, Jacob and Rebecca. She stays in frequent contact with her birth daughter, Stacey.

PAPIER-MACHE PRESS

At Papier-Mache Press, it is our goal to identify and successfully present important social issues through enduring works of beauty, grace, and strength. Through our work we hope to encourage empathy and respect among diverse communities, creating a bridge of understanding between the mainstream audience and those who might not otherwise be heard.

We appreciate you, our customer, and strive to earn your continued support. We also value the role of the bookseller in achieving our goals. We are especially grateful to the many independent booksellers whose presence ensures a continuing diversity of opinion, information, and literature in our communities. We encourage you to support these bookstores with your patronage.

We publish many fine books about women's experiences. We also produce lovely posters and T-shirts that complement our anthologies. Please ask your local bookstore which Papier-Mache items they carry. To receive our complete catalog, send your request to Papier-Mache Press, 135 Aviation Way, #14, Watsonville, CA 95076, or call our toll-free number, 800-927-5913.